Brazil

STEVE GOLDSWORTHY

MEDIA ENHANCED BOOKS
AV2 BY WEIGL
ADDED VALUE · AUDIO VISUAL

www.av2books.com

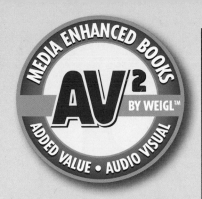

AV² provides enriched content that supplements and complements this book. Weigl's AV² books strive to create inspired learning and engage young minds in a total learning experience.

Your AV² Media Enhanced books come alive with...

Audio
Listen to sections of the book read aloud.

Key Words
Study vocabulary, and complete a matching word activity.

Video
Watch informative video clips.

Quizzes
Test your knowledge.

Go to **www.av2books.com**, and enter this book's unique code.

BOOK CODE

D 7 8 7 5 0 9

Embedded Weblinks
Gain additional information for research.

Slide Show
View images and captions, and prepare a presentation.

AV² by Weigl brings you media enhanced books that support active learning.

Try This!
Complete activities and hands-on experiments.

... and much, much more!

Published by AV² by Weigl
350 5th Avenue, 59th Floor
New York, NY 10118
Website: www.av2books.com   www.weigl.com

Library of Congress Cataloging-in-Publication Data

Goldsworthy, Steve.
  Brazil / Steve Goldsworthy.
    p. cm. — (Exploring countries)
  ISBN 978-1-62127-250-2 (hardcover : alk. paper) — ISBN 978-1-62127-256-4 (softcover : alk. paper)
  1. Brazil—Juvenile literature. I. Title.
  F2508.5.G637 2013   981—dc23

Printed in the United States of America in North Mankato, Minnesota
1 2 3 4 5 6 7 8 9 17 16 15 14 13

052013
WEP040413

Project Coordinator Heather Kissock
Art Director Terry Paulhus

Contents

Brazil Overview

Brazil, located on the continent of South America, is a country of diverse people and geography. It is home to the largest rainforest on Earth, as well as busy cities, such as Rio de Janeiro and São Paulo. **Indigenous** peoples in Brazil live in some of the most remote places in the world. Yet, Brazil, with its rich natural resources and active workforce, has one of the fastest-growing modern economies.

Brazil is home to many indigenous peoples, including the Kaiowa.

Green-winged macaws live in Brazil's tropical rainforests.

The *Cristo Redentor*, or "Christ the Redeemer," statue stands 98 feet (30 meters) tall on top of Mount Corcovado in Rio de Janeiro.

Brazil gets its name from a tree called *pau-brasil* in Portuguese. This tree, sometimes called brazilwood, is used to make cabinets and violin bows. Its seeds are red.

The capital city of Brasília features many modern buildings designed by Brazilian architect Oscar Niemeyer. The National Museum of the Republic, opened in 2006, has a long sloping ramp and four floors of art inside its white dome.

INDIGENOUS PEOPLES

Many different groups of indigenous peoples live in Brazil. When Portuguese explorers first arrived in Brazil in the beginning of the 16ᵗʰ century, most of the area's indigenous people belonged to **nomadic** tribes. At that time, more than 2,000 native groups lived in Brazil. Since then, many indigenous people died from diseases introduced by European settlers. Others were captured as slaves. Some had children with European settlers. The result was the loss of hundreds of these indigenous groups.

One of the main indigenous groups, the Tupi, had an estimated population of 1 million. They were farmers, growing corn, **cassava**, sweet potatoes, tobacco, and cotton. Many present-day Brazilians have one or more Tupi ancestors.

Today, the largest indigenous group in the Brazilian Amazon is the Ticuna. Most Ticuna people avoid contact with visitors. They prefer to preserve a way of life they have had for centuries. A government body called the National Indian Foundation works to protect lands traditionally inhabited and used by the country's indigenous peoples. Its 2007 report said Brazil has 67 different isolated tribes. An isolated tribe lives without any major contact with the rest of the world.

The Kayapo people live in the western state of Mato Grosso. Traditions such as the sacred-fire lighting ceremony continue to take place in the village of Kari-Oca.

36,377
Number of Ticuna living in Brazil, according to a 2009 report.

About 300,000
Total number of indigenous people in Brazil.

35 Million Acres
Size of isolated Indians' territory that the Brazilian government is working to protect.
(14 million ha)

Exploring Brazil

With a total area of 3,287,612 square miles (8,514,877 square kilometers), Brazil is the largest nation in the **Southern Hemisphere**. It is also the fifth-largest country in the world. Only Russia, Canada, the United States, and China cover more land. The Atlantic Ocean lies to the east of Brazil. The country's coastline is 4,603 miles (7,408 km) long. Brazil has both **lowlands** in the north and **highlands** in the southeast.

Venezuela

Guya

Colombia

Ecuador

Peru

Amazon Rainforest

Bolivia

Amazon Rainforest

Amazon River

Chile

Paraguay

Argentina

N

Map Legend

Brazil

Land

Water

Amazon River

Amazon Rainforest

Capital City

Brazilian Highlands

SCALE 500 Kilometers

500 Miles

Suriname

French
Guiana

BRAZIL

Brasília

Brasília

Brazilian Highlands

Amazon River

The Amazon River flows for more than 2,000 miles (3,300 km) through Brazil. It carries as much as 11 million cubic feet (300,000 cubic meters) of water per second to the Atlantic Ocean. That is more than any other river in the world.

Brasília

Brasília is the capital city of Brazil. Its population is 3.8 million, but it is not the country's largest city. São Paulo, Rio de Janeiro, and Belo Horizonte have many more residents.

Brazilian Highlands

This region covers much of Brazil. Some of the area's rolling hills and **plateaus** reach more than 4,000 feet (1,200 m) above sea level.

LAND AND CLIMATE

Brazil spans 2,731 miles (4,395 km) from north to south and 2,684 miles (4,319 km) from east to west. The country has a varied **topography**. It includes rolling hills, vast plains, mountain ranges, high plateaus, and low-lying land. About half of Brazil's land is less than 650 feet (200 m) above sea level. Brazil's coast is covered with tropical beaches, **lagoons**, and sand dunes. Brazil also has many **archipelagos** just off its coast. They include Fernando de Noronha, Saint Peter and Saint Paul Rocks, and Trindade and Martim Vaz.

Brazil's lowlands provide fertile soil for growing soybeans, corn, and sugarcane.

The northeast region of Brazil is the driest part of the country. During the dry season, between May and November, temperatures can reach 104° F (40° C). The Brazilian highlands are in the southeast. Rugged mountain ranges in this region include the Espinhaço, Mantiqueira, and Serra do Mar. In the far south, snow sometimes falls in the winter months. The central region of Brazil is a tropical **savanna** of grasslands and few trees. An average of 31 inches (79 centimeters) of rain falls here per year.

The Amazon basin in the north and west of Brazil is the world's largest drainage basin. A drainage basin is an area from which all rainwater flows to a river or a group of rivers. The rainforest in the Amazon basin gets as much as 120 inches (300 cm) of rain a year.

The Fernando de Noronha archipelago is made up of 21 islands in the Atlantic Ocean.

Land and Climate BY THE NUMBERS

9,823 Feet
Elevation of Pico da Neblina, the highest point in Brazil. (2,994 m)

35 Miles
Width of the Amazon River in some parts of Brazil. (55 km)

2 Number of South American countries that do not border Brazil. (Chile and Ecuador)

PLANTS AND ANIMALS

Brazil has a wide variety of plant and animal **species**. Scientists estimate that the entire Amazon rainforest has more than 40,000 plant species. It is also home to 427 mammal, more than 400 **amphibian**, 378 **reptile**, and 1,300 bird species. About 3,000 types of fish live in the rainforest's fresh water.

Big cats such as the jaguar and the cougar hunt throughout Brazil's jungles. Howler and squirrel monkeys, capuchins, and marmosets swing in the **canopy** of the rainforest. Snakes called anacondas and water boas move through the Amazon River. The river is home to the small but ferocious piranha, the electric eel, and the bull shark.

Giant anteaters and bush dogs roam the jungles and savannas. Marsh deer can be found in the southern regions. There are also poisonous dart frogs. They produce a toxin on their skin that can mean death to humans.

Other animals found in Brazil include the three-banded armadillo, the painted tree rat, the Santa Catarina's guinea pig, and the capybara. Capybaras are the world's largest rodents. Brazilian birds include parrots, flamingos, toucans, macaws, ducks, hawks, eagles, and hummingbirds.

175 Pounds
Weight of the largest capybaras. (80 kilograms)

1 in 5
Portion of the world's fish species that swim in the Amazon River or smaller rivers that empty into the Amazon.

70
Number of parrot species that live in Brazil.

160 Feet

Height that a Brazil nut tree can grow. (50 m)

The common toucan lives high in the canopy of the Amazon and feeds mostly on fruit.

NATURAL RESOURCES

Brazil is rich in natural resources. This vast country has plenty of forests, fresh water, and minerals. One of its challenges is managing these natural resources.

Trees are one of the most important natural resources in Brazil. Deforestation is the loss of large areas of forest. This is because the trees are cut down for lumber or cut and burned to clear the land for other uses. In Brazil, thousands of acres (hectares) of land are cleared every year to in order to plant crops and graze cattle. Almost 230,000 square miles (600,000 sq. km) of rainforest have disappeared since 1970. That area is almost as large as the country of France.

Brazil is among the biggest producers of iron ore in the world. One of its largest customers is China. Brazil is also rich in gold, nickel, phosphates, diamonds, limestone, and uranium. In recent years, Brazil has become a major producer of petroleum. Experts say it should be one of the world's top-five oil producers by 2020.

430 Million
Number of tons of iron ore produced by Brazil in a year. (390 million tonnes)

20%
Percentage of oxygen in Earth's atmosphere produced by trees and other types of plants in the Amazon rainforest.

100 Years
Predicted time it could take the Amazon rainforest to disappear if deforestation continues at the current rate.

Oil production platforms float in Guanabara Bay near Rio de Janeiro. Brazil's state-controlled oil company, Petrobras, has several rigs in the bay.

TOURISM

Brazil has become a popular tourist destination for people all around the world. In 2011, 5.4 million people visited the country. The only South American country with more international tourists is Argentina.

Visitors to Rio de Janeiro, which is often called Rio, can ride a cable car up Sugarloaf Mountain or enjoy the Sun and surf on one of the city's 23 beaches. Most Rio hotels are on the beaches of Ipanema and Copacabana. Rio tourists can see the breathtaking view from the foot of the Christ the Redeemer statue. Completed in 1931, it is visible from almost anywhere in the city. Many people come to Rio for the celebration known as Carnival, which often takes place in February.

Tourists in Brazil have been flocking to the northeastern state of Bahia for decades. Visitors can explore the sandy beaches, crystal-clear bays, and colorful coral reefs along the coast. The many beaches and resort towns that line other parts of the east coast are also popular. In the highlands, there are mountain parks for hiking, rafting, and kayaking.

Saudade Island, near Morro de São Paulo in the state of Bahia, is considered one of the most beautiful beaches in Brazil.

More than 40 million people have traveled to the top of Sugarloaf Mountain by cable car.

One of Brazil's greatest tourist attractions is the Amazon rainforest. Many people come to the country as ecotourists. They want to see and learn about the ecosystem of this natural area, as well as find out about **conservation** efforts. People can take cruises on the Amazon River to view the region's beauty and its variety of plant and animal life.

Another attraction for visitors to Brazil is Iguaçu Falls, on the border between the Brazilian state of Paraná and Argentina's province of Misiones. The waters of the Iguaçu River flow over a breathtaking series of waterfalls. The name *Iguaçu* comes from the Tupi word for *water*. The Tupi were one of the largest groups of indigenous peoples in Brazil. The falls have been declared a World Heritage Site by **UNESCO**.

The Iguaçu Falls span about 1.7 miles (2.7 km) across. Rocks and growths of trees divide the river into more than 250 separate waterfalls.

Tourism BY THE NUMBERS

$6.6 BILLION
Brazil's income from tourism each year.

44
Number of Brazil's national parks.

More Than 2,500
Number of museums in Brazil.

INDUSTRY

The rapid growth of its industries makes Brazil a powerful emerging, or developing, economy. Brazil has the seventh-largest economy of any country, based on its gross domestic product, or GDP. That is the total value of all goods and services produced in a year.

Brazil's industry began to develop in the 19th century. Small factories in the southeast made soap, candles, and wool and silk fabrics. At this time, the country was also producing rubber and minerals.

Today, Brazil is one of the world's largest producers of motor vehicles and parts. European, American, and Japanese auto companies have factories in Brazil. More than three million cars and trucks are made in Brazil each year.

The energy industry in Brazil is also thriving. As of 2006, Brazil no longer needed to import oil from foreign countries. More than 85 percent of its energy comes from renewable sources. These are sources, such as sunlight and water power, that will not run out. They also include sources such as plants that can be grown again in a short period of time. Brazil relies on **hydroelectricity** to provide energy.

Brazil is the second-largest producer of ethanol fuel in the world, after the United States. Brazil's ethanol fuel is made by processing sugarcane. In 2011, Brazil produced more than 5.5 billion gallons (21 billion liters) of ethanol. Much of this fuel is used in cars and trucks.

Itaipu Dam on the Paraná River, a joint project with Paraguay, is Brazil's largest hydroelectric facility. It is also one of the world's biggest dams.

GOODS AND SERVICES

Brazil provides its own people and the world with many goods and services. Besides automobiles, Brazil produces aircraft, computers and computer chips, and electronics products, including televisions, DVD players, and cell phones. There is also a large textile industry, making yarn and fabric. The biggest customers for Brazil's **exports** are the United States, Colombia, Japan, Germany, Argentina, China, Canada, and the United Kingdom.

Farmers in Brazil grow, harvest, and sell various agricultural products. The country is the world's number-one producer of coffee and sugarcane. It is also the world's largest grower of oranges. Brazil produces more soybeans than any other country except the United States. Its other exports include wheat, rice, cocoa, corn, and beef.

More than 100 million of Brazil's residents have jobs. Most of the country's workers are employed in service industries. These people have jobs in tourism businesses. People who work in service industries also teach, care for sick people, collect trash, and deliver mail. They work in insurance, banking, air transportation, and energy distribution.

Brazil's restaurants, cafés, and food stands employ many of the country's service industry workers.

Goods and Services BY THE NUMBERS

MORE THAN 65%
Percentage of Brazil's workers who earn their living in the service industries.

1727
Year the first coffee bush was planted in Brazil.

Almost 1 in 6

Glasses of Brazilian orange juice consumed in the United States.

THE AGE OF EXPLORATION

Portuguese navigator Pedro Álvares Cabral claimed Brazil for Portugal on April 22, 1500. Cabral and his crew met some of the Tupi people, who treated the newcomers peacefully. Two days later, Cabral and his fleet landed at what is now Porto Seguro, which means "safe harbor" in Portuguese.

The Portuguese soon discovered the vast forest of brazilwood trees in the northeast region of the country. The trees were valued for their soft wood and for the red dye in them. The local people worked for the Portuguese, logging the forests in exchange for European goods such as knives, axes, mirrors, and scissors.

A group of explorers and slave hunters called bandeirantes carried out much of the early exploration of Brazil. Led by Europeans, they captured indigenous people and sold them to owners of sugarcane farms on the east coast in the 16th century. These bandeirantes also explored unmapped land looking for gold, diamonds, and silver. The actions of the bandeirantes were often cruel. However, these explorers helped increase European knowledge and control of the vast Brazilian interior.

1530s
Decade the first sugarcane farms were established.

13 Number of ships Pedro Álvares Cabral sailed to today's Brazil.

Pedro Álvares Cabral of Portugal landed on the coast of what is now Brazil in 1500. Today, Brazil is the largest Portuguese-speaking country in the world.

EARLY SETTLERS

Many scientists believe Brazil's indigenous groups descended from others who came to America from North Asia at the end of the last Ice Age. About 15,000 years ago, these people began crossing a strip of land. This strip of land, which is now underwater, connected Russia and Alaska. Over time, these travelers and their descendants spread out to live in almost all parts of North and South America. The earliest people to live in what is now Brazil survived for thousands of years by hunting, fishing, and gathering fruits and herbs for food.

Traditional clothing of the Bahia region includes colorful turbans and earrings.

After Portugal claimed what is now Brazil, Portuguese settlers began to arrive in sizable numbers in the early 1530s. A Portuguese soldier named Tomé de Sousa became the first governor-general of the **colony** in 1549. From Portugal, he brought several Jesuit priests to spread the Christian religion to the indigenous people. Sousa established Salvador as the capital city in the eastern region of Bahia. Many of the other early settlers from Portugal were criminals. Sousa established peaceful relations with many of the indigenous groups and brought order to the colony of Brazil.

Salvador is one of Brazil's oldest cities. The historic center of the former capital city includes cobblestoned streets and colonial architecture.

By the early 1600s, many groups, including the French, Dutch, English, and Irish, attempted to settle regions in Brazil. The Portuguese remained in control, however. Portuguese settlers brought slaves from Africa to work the sugarcane fields. Later, slaves were used on coffee farms as well. After slavery was officially ended in Brazil in 1888, many former slaves moved to cities such as Rio de Janeiro.

In the late 1800s, a large number of European settlers arrived in Brazil. At least half of them went to southern regions to farm. They were mainly Germans and Italians. Other new settlers, including people from Italy, Portugal, and Spain, worked on the coffee **plantations** in the southeast. Many people also came to Brazil from Japan in the late 1800s and early 1900s.

Harvesting coffee remains an important industry in Brazil. Today, the country accounts for about one-third of the world's production of coffee beans.

1/3 Estimate of the portion of Brazilians who have some Indian ancestors.

1630 to 1654
Years the Dutch ruled the port city of Recife in northeastern Brazil until the Portuguese regained control.

POPULATION

With more than 200 million residents, Brazil is the fifth-most-populated country in the world. Most Brazilians live in urban areas. Brazil's largest city, São Paulo, has a population of almost 20 million. The next-largest city, Rio de Janeiro, has a population of just under 12 million. Farther north, about 5.5 million people live in Brazil's third-biggest city, Belo Horizonte. The most densely populated parts of the country are along the eastern coastline. Heavily forested regions in the west and north of Brazil have fewer than 30 million residents.

As a result of the country's growing economy, more people are arriving in Brazil every year. Many recent immigrants have come from Argentina, Chile, and other South American countries. Most of them move to the more developed southeastern part of Brazil. Despite economic improvements, many Brazilians still live in poverty. Some unskilled Brazilian workers leave to do agricultural work in nearby countries.

Overcrowded, poorly built housing covers the outskirts of Brazilian cities such as Rio de Janeiro. These settlements are called favelas.

Population BY THE NUMBERS

More Than 84%
Percentage of Brazilians who live in town or cities.

1/4 Portion of Brazilians who are under 15 years of age.

21% Percentage of Brazilians living in poverty.

MORE THAN 9/10
Portion of Brazilians age 15 and older who can read and write.

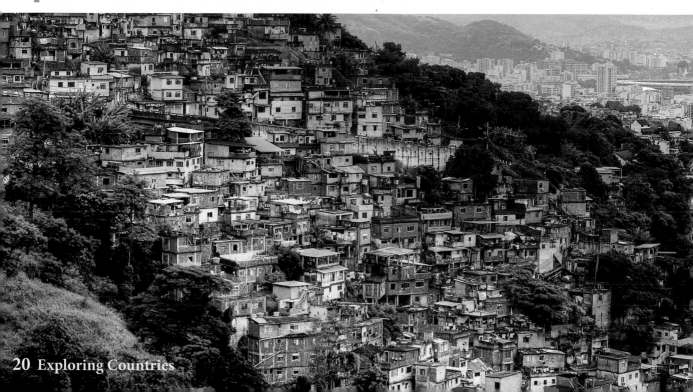

POLITICS AND GOVERNMENT

The French emperor Napoleon invaded Portugal in the early 1800s. In 1808, Portuguese ruler Dom João VI fled to Brazil. He set up a united kingdom of Portugal and Brazil in 1815. When Dom João VI returned to Portugal, he left his son Dom Pedro in charge of Brazil. Dom Pedro declared Brazil independent on September 7, 1822, and remained in power after several revolts. Portugal recognized Brazil as its own country in 1825.

Brazil experienced a great deal of political unrest in the 20th century. From the 1930s to the 1960s, many Brazilian governments were overthrown in **coups d'état**. Military **dictators** often ruled the country. Citizens lost many of their rights.

In 1988, the Constitution of the Federative **Republic** of Brazil went into effect. It provides for a democratic government. The document also protects the civil rights of every Brazilian citizen.

The modern country of Brazil is made up of 26 states and the federal district of Brasília, the national capital. Each state has several municipalities, governed by elected local officials. The country has an elected president, a congress, and a national court system. The National Congress, composed of the Chamber of Deputies and the Federal Senate, has elected members from each state and the federal district.

2011
Year Brazil's first woman president, Dilma Rousseff, took office.

September 7
Celebration of Independence Day in Brazil.

594
Number of members of the National Congress.

Brazil's Congress meets in the National Congress building, which opened in Brasília in 1958.

CULTURAL GROUPS

Portuguese is Brazil's official language.

Many different cultural groups make up the population of Brazil today. Most Brazilians are of European descent. Almost half of Brazilians have at least some African ancestors. African slaves brought their own cultures, religions, and languages to Brazil. Some of those slaves escaped and formed settlements known as quilombos, or maroons. These settlements were established in the northeast coastal region of Pernabuco. The city of Palmares began as one of these slave settlements.

Almost all Brazilians speak Portuguese. Language has helped to strengthen the country's unity. There are very few differences between the Portuguese spoken in different regions of the country. This lack of regional differences is unusual when a language is spoken in such a vast country. Speaking the same language helps different cultural groups communicate and work together.

African traditions have influenced Brazil's culture. Salvador's local art, with vibrant colors and traditional scenes, reflects that influence.

A number of Brazilians can speak or understand at least some Spanish. Portuguese is similar in some ways to Spanish, which is the main language spoken in almost all South American countries. Knowing some Spanish helps Brazilians communicate with their Spanish-speaking neighbors.

There are many indigenous languages spoken in Brazil. The language most widely spoken is Guaraní. It is based on the language of the Tupi people. In the central Mato Grosso region, Bororo is spoken by an indigenous group with the same name. Kaingang is spoken by people in the southeast region around São Paulo.

A number of different religions are practiced in Brazil. Almost three-quarters of Brazilians are Roman Catholic. The next-largest religious group is Protestants. Some people follow indigenous or traditional African beliefs. They may combine these with Christian beliefs. About seven percent of Brazilians follow no religion at all.

Although most of its people are Catholic, Brazil has no official religion.

Cultural Groups BY THE NUMBERS

5 MILLION
Number of African slaves brought to Brazil.

15% Percentage of Brazilians who are Protestant.

180 Number of indigenous languages spoken in Brazil.

ARTS AND ENTERTAINMENT

Carnival is the most-celebrated holiday in Brazil. Forty days before Easter, the entire country stops almost completely for the week. Festivals, held mainly in coastal cities, run day and night. People parade in the streets dressed in colorful costumes. They dance and sing traditional Brazilian music. People ride spectacular floats and wear feather headgear.

Brazilian musicians often play a handheld drum called a pandeiro.

Samba has come to represent Brazil, especially at Carnival. This kind of dance originated in Bahia in the early 1900s. It came out of Brazilian and African roots. Samba musicians play guitars, trombones, trumpets, and saxophones. They also use instruments such as drums, cowbells, rattles, and whistles. Other Brazilian styles of dance and music include zouk-lambada, bossa nova, frevo, and forró.

Samba performers of all ages participate in Carnival parades.

Capoeira is a Brazilian martial art that combines music and dance. Male dancers spin, whirl, and kick. The activity was brought to Brazil by its African slaves. Instruments and call-and-response singing accompany the dances, which are performed by men and women.

Brazilian art is a mixture of Portuguese, African, and indigenous cultures. Many pieces of art with highly detailed carvings and paintings of animals and plants have been discovered. Indigenous people on the island of Marajó at the mouth of the Amazon River created stunning works of pottery beginning around the year 800. Many indigenous groups in Brazil continue the traditional art form of body painting and feather art.

Capoeira features staged fighting stances, defensive postures, and attacking jabs.

SPORTS

The people of Brazil participate in and enjoy watching a variety of sports. Many of them are world-class athletes. Soccer, called football in Brazil and many other parts of the world, is the country's most popular sport. The International Federation of Association Football (FIFA) ranks Brazil's national men's and women's teams as some of the best in the world. The men's team has won the World Cup tournament a record five times. It is the only team to have qualified for every FIFA World Cup since the worldwide competition began in 1930. Brazil is set to host the 2014 FIFA men's World Cup.

Pelé averaged one goal per international game during his career.

One of the all-time superstars of soccer is the Brazilian player Pelé. Respected as a national hero, Pelé led his country to three World Cup championships, in 1958, 1962, and 1970. He began playing professionally at age 15, and he won his first World Cup at age 17.

Marta is another Brazilian soccer superstar. As her team's top-scoring player, she has helped make Brazil the best women's national soccer team in South America. She has also played for professional clubs in Brazil, the United States, and Sweden. Marta was named the FIFA women's world player of the year five times in a row, from 2006 to 2010.

Marta has been an inspiring example for girls who play soccer in Brazil.

Brazil also dominates in the sport of volleyball. Its men's and women's volleyball teams have won many international competitions. Their victories include two Olympic gold medals each.

Brazil developed its own style of martial art in the 1910s. Brazilian jiu-jitsu was a form of the original Japanese jujitsu. It emphasizes ground-fighting techniques and several new holds.

Ayrton Senna was a Brazilian Formula One race car driver. He won three Formula One World Championships. Tragically, he was killed during the 1994 San Marino Grand Prix race.

Basketball is a very popular sport in Brazil. The Brazilian national team won the Basketball World Championship in 1959 and in 1963. Brazilians often play in the National Basketball Association in the United States.

The Brazilian women's volleyball team won the gold medal at the 2012 London Olympics.

Sports BY THE NUMBERS

1992
First year the country of Brazil took part in the Winter Olympics.

SEVEN
Number of Wimbledon and U.S. Open singles tennis championships that Maria Bueno of Brazil won from 1959 to 1966.

2016
Year that Brazil becomes the first South American country to host the Summer Olympics.

Mapping Brazil

W e use many tools to interpret maps and to understand the locations of features such as cities, states, lakes, and rivers. The map below has many tools to help interpret information on the map of Brazil.

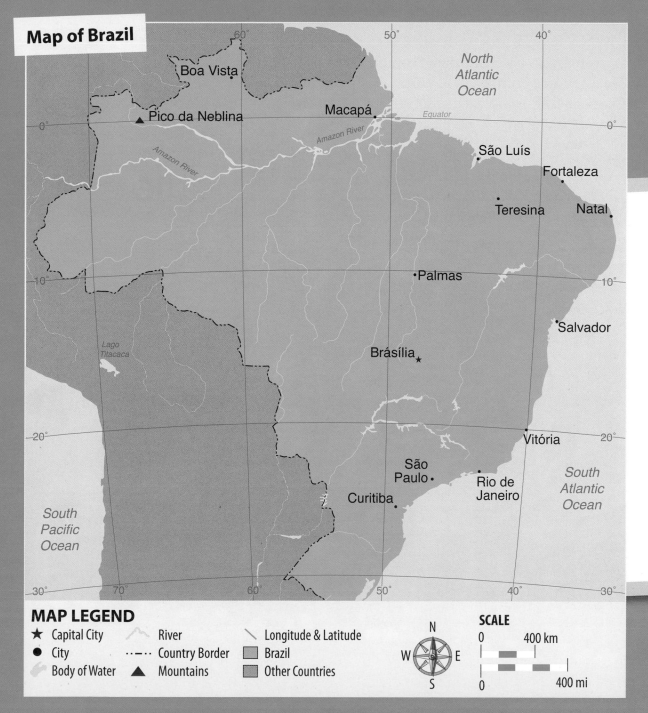

Map of Brazil

Boa Vista

Pico da Neblina

Macapá

North Atlantic Ocean

Equator

Amazon River

Amazon River

São Luís

Fortaleza

Teresina

Natal

Palmas

Salvador

Lago Titicaca

Brásília

Vitória

São Paulo

Rio de Janeiro

South Atlantic Ocean

Curitiba

South Pacific Ocean

MAP LEGEND

★ Capital City
● City
Body of Water

River
-·-·- Country Border
▲ Mountains

Longitude & Latitude
Brazil
Other Countries

N W E S

SCALE
0   400 km

0   400 mi

Mapping Tools

- The compass rose shows north, south, east, and west. The points in between represent northeast, northwest, southeast, and southwest.
- The map scale shows that the distances on a map represent much longer distances in real life. If you measure the distance between objects on a map, you can use the map scale to calculate the actual distance in miles or kilometers between those two points.

- The lines of latitude and longitude are long lines that appear on maps. The lines of latitude run east to west and measure how far north or south of the equator a place is located. The lines of longitude run north to south and measure how far east or west of the Prime Meridian a place is located. A location on a map can be found by using the two numbers where latitude and longitude meet. This number is called a coordinate and is written using degrees and direction. For example, the city of Los Angeles would be found at 34°N and 118°W on a map.

Map It!

Using the map and the appropriate tools, complete the activities below.

Locating with latitude and longitude

1. What northern Brazilian city is located exactly on the equator at 51°W?
2. What city has the coordinates 20°S and 40°W?
3. What mountain is located at 0° and 66°W?

Distances between points

4. Using the map scale and a ruler, calculate the approximate distance between the cities of Brasília and Rio de Janeiro.
5. What is the approximate width of Brazil from its westernmost border to the Atlantic Ocean?
6. Using the map scale and a ruler, find the approximate length of Brazil from its northernmost to its southernmost point.

Quiz Time

Test your knowledge of Brazil by answering these questions.

1 In what year did Portugal claim Brazil?

2 About what percentage of the Amazon rainforest is in Brazil?

3 How much of the Amazon rainforest has been deforested since 1970?

4 Which kind of tree gave the country of Brazil its name?

5 What is the current population of Brazil?

6 How much of the oxygen in Earth's atmosphere comes from trees and other plants in the Amazon rainforest?

7 What percentage of Brazil's energy comes from renewable sources?

8 What is the name of the largest group of indigenous people living in the Brazilian Amazon today?

9 What is the name of the first female president of Brazil?

10 Who was named the FIFA women's world player of the year five times in a row?

ANSWERS

1. 1500
2. 60 percent
3. 230,000 square miles (600,000 sq. km)
4. The *pau-brasil* or brazilwood tree
5. More than 200 million
6. 20 percent
7. More than 85 percent
8. The Ticuna
9. Dilma Rousseff
10. Marta

Key Words

amphibian: an animal that lives both on land and in the water

archipelagos: large groups of islands

canopy: the layer of branches at the tops of trees in a forest

cassava: the root of a tropical tree used for food

colony: land outside its borders that a country claims and governs

conservation: the act of protecting, preserving, managing, or restoring wildlife and natural resources

coups d'état: sudden overthrows of a government, bringing new groups into power

dictators: leaders who have complete power over their people and who may govern in a cruel or unfair way

ecosystem: a biological community where all life forms exist together and depend on one another

exports: goods or products that are sent to another country for trade or sale

highlands: elevated lands

hydroelectricity: electricity produced using the energy of moving water, such as in a river or ocean waves

indigenous: native to a particular area

lagoons: shallow bodies of coastal water separated from the sea

lowlands: areas of low, flat land

nomadic: related to a people who move around in search of food, water, and other needs

plantations: large farms that grow crops to be sold and that often are worked by people who live on the farm

plateaus: high flat areas of land

reptile: a cold-blooded animal that has a backbone, scales or horny plates, and lungs, such as lizards, snakes, and turtles

republic: a political state in which the people vote their head of state into office

savanna: a flat area of land covered with grass and a few trees

Southern Hemisphere: the half of Earth south of the equator

species: groups of individuals with common characteristics

topography: the arrangement of natural features on a landscape

UNESCO: the United Nations Educational, Scientific, and Cultural Organization whose main goals are to promote world peace and eliminate poverty through education, science, and culture

Index

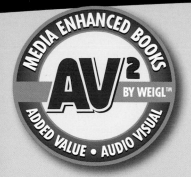

Log on to www.av2books.com

AV² by Weigl brings you media enhanced books that support active learning. Go to www.av2books.com, and enter the special code found on page 2 of this book. You will gain access to enriched and enhanced content that supplements and complements this book. Content includes video, audio, weblinks, quizzes, a slide show, and activities.

AV² Online Navigation

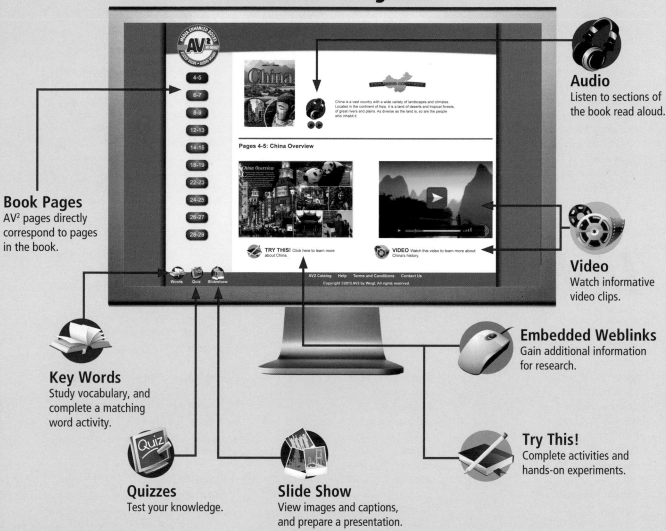

Audio
Listen to sections of the book read aloud.

Book Pages
AV² pages directly correspond to pages in the book.

Video
Watch informative video clips.

Key Words
Study vocabulary, and complete a matching word activity.

Embedded Weblinks
Gain additional information for research.

Try This!
Complete activities and hands-on experiments.

Quizzes
Test your knowledge.

Slide Show
View images and captions, and prepare a presentation.

AV² was built to bridge the gap between print and digital. We encourage you to tell us what you like and what you want to see in the future.

Sign up to be an AV² Ambassador at www.av2books.com/ambassador.

Due to the dynamic nature of the Internet, some of the URLs and activities provided as part of AV² by Weigl may have changed or ceased to exist. AV² by Weigl accepts no responsibility for any such changes. All media enhanced books are regularly monitored to update addresses and sites in a timely manner. Contact AV² by Weigl at 1-866-649-3445 or av2books@weigl.com with any questions, comments, or feedback.